MISSOURI

in words and pictures

BY DENNIS B. FRADIN

ILLUSTRATIONS BY RICHARD WAHL

MAPS BY LEN W. MEENTS

Consultant
Gary N. Smith
Curator of Museum Collections
Missouri Historical Society
St. Louis

 CHILDRENS PRESS, CHICAGO

For my friend, Robert Wilcox

Turtle Island

Fradin, Dennis B
  Missouri in words and pictures.

  SUMMARY: A brief introduction to the history, land,
cities, industries, and famous citizens and sites in the Show Me State.
  1. Missouri—Juvenile literature. [1. Missouri]
I. Wahl, Richard, 1939- II. Title.
F466.3.F7   977.8   80-12249
ISBN 0-516-03925-3

1 2 3 4 5 6 7 8 9 10 11 12 R 87 86 85 84 83 82 81 80

Picture Acknowledgments:
CONVENTION AND VISITORS BUREAU OF GREATER ST. LOUIS—
cover, 8, 20 (right), 24 (left), 25, 26 (left and center)
WALKER-MISSOURI DIVISION OF TOURISM—2, 4, 16, 19, 21, 24
(right), 26 (right), 28, 29, 31, 32, 33, 34, 35, 36, 37, 38, 39, 41 (left)
JAMES P. ROWAN—20 (left), 41 (right)
INTERNATIONAL HARVESTER—23
COVER PICTURE—St. Louis waterfront

Missouri

The word *Missouri* (mih • ZOO • ree) is thought to come from an Indian word that means "town of the large canoes." The Missouri were an Indian tribe. The river where they lived was called the Missouri River. The state was given the name, too.

Missouri is near the middle of the United States. Rich soils make it a leading farming state. Rivers and hills make it beautiful. Missouri also has big cities like St. Louis (LOO • iss) and Kansas City.

Do you know the home state of our 33rd president, Harry S. Truman? What state has a big city founded by a 14-year-old boy? Where did the outlaw Jesse James live and die? Where is the country's tallest monument— the Gateway Arch? As you will learn, the answer to these questions is: Missouri, the *Show Me State.*

3

About 8,000 years ago, Indians used Graham Cave.

About 200 million years ago dinosaurs roamed the land. Their bones have been found in Missouri.

About one million years ago the Ice Age began. Mountains of ice, called *glaciers*, (GLAY • shurz) covered northern Missouri. Glaciers flattened the land. They ground up rocks into rich soil. This helped northern Missouri become a fine farming area.

The first people came to Missouri at least 10,000 years ago. Their stone tools, weapons, and pottery have been found in such places as Graham (GRAY • um) Cave. Tools serve as clues about the ancient people. They fished and hunted. They learned to farm.

One early group is called the Mound Builders. They built dirt hills—called mounds—throughout a big area of America. Some mounds were used to bury the dead. Others were forts. One mound, near Caruthersville (kah • RUH • therz • vill) is 400 feet long.

Modern Indians may be related to the Mound Builders. Many Indian tribes lived in Missouri. The Missouri, Fox, Sauk, (SAWK) and Osage (oh • SAGE) were four tribes in the area. Some Osage were known to walk 50 miles a day through their hunting grounds.

The Indians planted corn, beans, and pumpkins in the spring. Summer rains helped the crops grow. Then the Indians hunted deer, elk, and buffalo. The people ate the meat. They used the skins to make clothes and moccasins. In the fall the Indians returned from hunting. They harvested their crops. Then they hunted bears and beavers until the winter snows.

The Spanish explorer De Soto may have entered Missouri in 1541. The French were the first known explorers there. In 1673 two Frenchmen paddled down the Mississippi River. Their names were Louis Joliet (joe • lee • YAY) and Jacques Marquette (ZHAK mar • KETT). Marquette was a priest. Joliet was a fur trader. The two men came to the mouth of the Missouri River. They met with friendly Indians.

Another Frenchman, La Salle (la SAL), paddled down the Mississippi River in 1682. La Salle claimed a large area for the King of France. This included Missouri.

Missouri had treasures that Frenchmen wanted. These were animal furs. There were millions of beavers and otters. The furs of these animals were worth a lot of money. They were made into fancy clothes. French fur trappers arrived in Missouri. They caught the animals themselves. Fur traders came, too. They traded pots, beads, and trinkets to the Indians. In return they received animal furs.

French priests, called *missionaries*, arrived. They wanted to turn the Indians into Christians. In 1700 they founded a church near present-day St. Louis. It was called Mission of St. Francis Xavier (ZAY • vyur). The mission lasted just a few years.

French miners arrived in the early 1700s. They mined lead—used to make bullets. A few Illinois (ILL • ih • noy) farmers moved across the Mississippi River. In about 1735 the town of Ste. Genevieve (SAINT JEN • ah • veev) was built. It was near lead mines and farms. Ste. Genevieve is the oldest town in Missouri. You can see houses built in the 1700s in this Mississippi River town.

Ste. Genevieve, the oldest town in Missouri

In 1763 a fur trader, Pierre Lacléde (pee • AIR lah • KLEED), traveled up the Mississippi River with his stepson. Lacléde was looking for a place to build a trading post. He chose land near the Mississippi River. Frenchmen and Indians could come here by canoe. Next spring Lacléde sent his stepson, René Auguste Chouteau (reh • NAY oh • GOOST shoo • TOE). Chouteau started building the trading post. The town that grew into St. Louis was begun. Chouteau was only 14 years old!

Families began to settle in Missouri. They built log cabins and grew corn. Daniel Boone lost his land in Kentucky (ken • TUCK • ee). So he decided to settle in Missouri. His family went there by boat. But 65-year-old Daniel Boone walked there. On the way, people asked him why he was going so far into the wilderness. "I want more elbowroom!" Boone said.

From 1762-1800 Spain took control of Missouri. Then, in 1800 France regained control. But not for long. A new country—the United States of America—had been formed in 1776. In 1803 the United States bought a large piece of land from France. Missouri was included.

President Thomas Jefferson wanted to learn about the land the United States now owned. Meriwether Lewis (MER • e • weh • thur LOO • iss) and William Clark explored the Missouri River area from 1804-1806. They learned that Missouri had great farmland. They saw that rivers allowed people to travel there by boat. Meriwether Lewis later became a governor of the Missouri Territory.

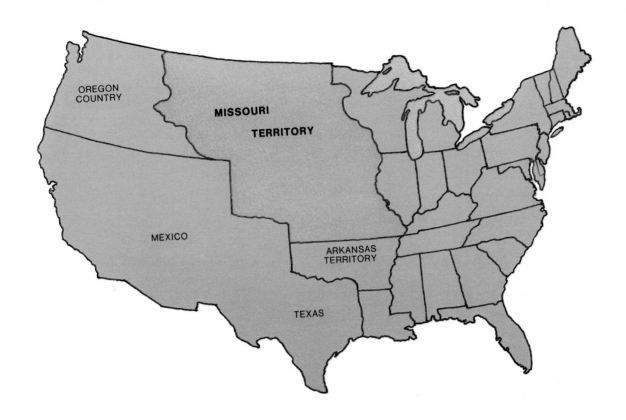

It was in 1812 that Missouri became a territory. It wasn't a state yet. The Missouri Territory was land owned by the United States.

There were many problems for the Missouri settlers. In 1811-1812 earthquakes shook southeastern Missouri. Houses were destroyed. The waters of the Mississippi River were hurled high into the sky. New lakes were formed by these waters. The shocks of the New Madrid earthquakes were felt 1,000 miles away.

There were troubles with the Indians. Often the lands the settlers took belonged to Indians. The Indians were forced out. You remember how the Osage Indians once walked 50 miles a day through their lands. They were sent onto a small piece of land outside Missouri. Other tribes were also made to sign away their lands. Some Indians fought. But they had no chance against U.S. soldiers. By 1815 the Indians were beaten. Today, only about 5,400 Indians live in the whole state.

With the Indian wars ended, thousands of settlers arrived in Missouri. Slavery was allowed in Missouri, just as it was in the South. Some farmers who came from the South brought black slaves. The slaves did the work on large farms, called *plantations* (plan • TAY • shuns).

Starting in 1818, many people wanted Missouri to become a state. At this time, eleven states allowed slavery. Eleven states didn't.

If Missouri became a Slave State, there would be more
Slave States than Free States. United States lawmakers
argued about it. Finally, Maine was admitted as a Free
State. Missouri was allowed to become a Slave State.
Keeping the balance between Slave and Free states was
part of what was called the Missouri Compromise.

It was August 10, 1821 when Missouri became the
24th state. Five years later, in 1826, Jefferson City was
made the capital of Missouri.

Americans turned animal furs into a giant business. John Jacob Astor opened an office of his American Fur Company in St. Louis. Furs were brought to St. Louis from many areas of America. The fur business just about wiped out beavers and otters. Other animals—such as bears, buffalo, and elk—were killed off by hunters.

Many people who had come to Missouri from the East were restless. As soon as Missouri was built up, they wanted to go farther into the wilderness. Trails were built west from Missouri. In about 1821 the Santa Fe Trail was built. It started in Independence, Missouri and led to Santa Fe, New Mexico. In about 1841 the Oregon

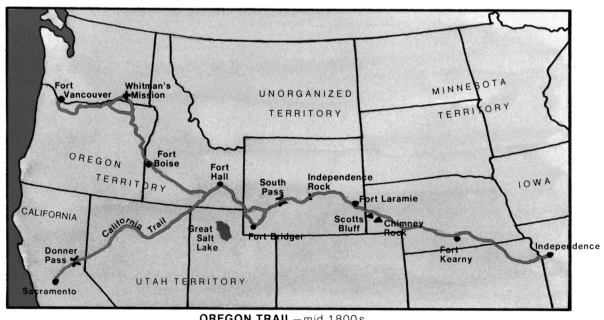

OREGON TRAIL—mid 1800s

(OR • eh • gon) Trail opened. It, too, started in
Independence. Families in covered wagons arrived. They
formed lines of wagons known as "wagon trains." Some
people went to farm in Oregon. Others went to California
(kal • eh • FORN • yah) in search of gold.

Because so many of the state's people settled the
West, Missouri was nicknamed the *Mother of the West.*

The Old Courthouse in St. Louis where Dred Scott was tried

In 1846 a Missouri slave named Dred Scott sued for his freedom. In 1857 the United States Supreme Court made the famous Dred Scott Decision. It said slaves had no right to even bring cases to court. Slaves were property, like horses. This angered people who disliked slavery.

Many Southerners feared that President Abraham Lincoln would soon end slavery. Many Northerners felt slavery *should* be ended. Northern and Southern people also argued about taxes and other issues.

The talking stopped. War between the Northern and Southern states began on April 12, 1861. This was the Civil War.

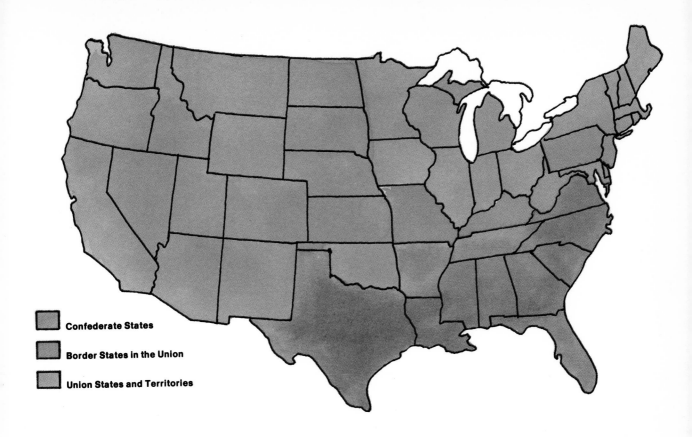

Confederate States

Border States in the Union

Union States and Territories

Although Missouri allowed slavery, the map shows that it wasn't a Southern state. It was a *border* state— between the North and the South. Some Missouri people wanted their state to fight on the side of the South. Others wanted it to be with the North.

Missouri people voted. They decided to join the North in its fight against the South. About 109,000 men joined the Northern, or Union (YOON • yun), army. But some Missourians—about 30,000—fought in the Southern, or Confederate (kahn • FED • er • it), army.

The Civil War was the bloodiest war in our nation's history. As a border state, Missouri suffered more than most states. There were fights in the streets of St. Louis between Missouri people. Raiders also entered the state. One, William Quantrill (kwan • TRILL), burned houses and killed pro-North people. There were also raids against those who supported the South.

Missouri had over 1,000 Civil War battles—more than any other state except Tennessee and Virginia. In August of 1861 Southern soldiers beat Northern soldiers at Wilson's Creek, near Springfield. But by 1864 Missouri was in the hands of the Northern army.

The Civil War ended in 1865. The North had won. That same year the slaves were freed in Missouri.

After the Civil War, those who had fought on the Southern side couldn't vote. They couldn't get jobs. A

The home of Jesse James

few became outlaws. Jesse James, born in Clay County, became a famous outlaw. He and his brother Frank James formed a gang with Cole Younger. Wearing masks, they robbed banks and trains. Jesse James made many daring getaways. The governor of Missouri offered $5,000 for his capture. Jesse James was shot and killed by one of his own men who wanted the reward.

The railroads—that Jesse James had so often robbed—became important. Flour, paint, and beer were made in St. Louis. Meat was packed in Kansas City. These goods went by train to cities across the U.S.

A Mississippi riverboat

The 1904 World's Fair

The way to travel on the rivers was by steamboat. In those days steamboats on the Mississippi and Missouri rivers were like floating palaces. Steamboats sometimes raced between New Orleans and St. Louis. In 1870, a race was held between the *Robert E. Lee* and the *Natchez*. The *Natchez* got lost in the fog. The *Robert E. Lee* won the race in under four days.

Missouri's nickname is the *Show Me State*. It is thought that Congressman Willard Duncan Vandiver (VAN • deh • veer) gave Missouri this nickname in 1899. Another congressman was bragging about his own state. Vandiver said: "I'm from Missouri and you've got to show me!" That was a nice way to say he didn't quite believe the bragging.

In 1904, people from around the world gathered in St. Louis. The world's fair was held there. "Meet me in St. Louis, Louis, Meet me at the Fair!" began a popular song at the time. People came to St. Louis to see a new invention—the automobile. "It'll never work!" said some. Another "invention" at the fair was quite tasty. This was the ice-cream cone!

Across the state from the world's fair lived a young man named Harry S. Truman. Truman had been born in a tiny house in Lamar on May 8, 1884. He moved to Independence at an early age. "Old Four Eyes"—as some children called him—read hundreds of books in the Independence library. Truman became a judge and then

The house where Harry S. Truman was born

a United States senator. He became known as an honest man of the people. In 1944 he was elected vice-president. When President Roosevelt died in 1945, Harry S. Truman became our 33rd president.

In 1948 Harry Truman ran for president on his own. Most people thought he had no chance. But Truman won. After his terms as president, Harry Truman returned to live the rest of his life in Independence, Missouri. The "people's president" died in 1972, in nearby Kansas City.

During Harry Truman's lifetime, Missouri became a great farming state. Today, it is known for growing soybeans. It is also a leading corn-growing state.

Missouri has become a leading manufacturing state. Many things are made in the factories of St. Louis, Kansas City, and other cities. Airplanes, cars, spaceships, beer, and shoes are some products made in Missouri.

Missouri is a great farming state.
Farms cover about 30 million acres of land.

You have learned about some of Missouri's history. Now it is time for a trip—in words and pictures— through the Show Me State.

From the air, Missouri is bright with color. There are winding blue rivers. In the southern half of the state, you'll see the green Ozark (OH • zark) Mountains. Much of the north looks like a green and yellow checkerboard. Soybeans and corn grow well on this flat land.

Your airplane is landing in a big city in the east. This is St. Louis. It is the largest city in the state. St. Louis rises above the banks of the Mississippi River.

Long ago, Missouri and Osage Indians lived by the river. Indian burial mounds were found here.

Left: Gateway Arch sits next to the Mississippi River.
Above: The inside of the St. Louis Arch Museum

Saint Louis was named after a King of France. Many French people live in St. Louis today. You'll also find blacks, Italians, Germans, and many other groups.

Visit the famous Gateway Arch in St. Louis. It is a rainbow-shaped monument next to the Mississippi River. The Gateway Arch was built to remind people that this region was once the gateway to the West.

The Gateway Arch is the tallest monument in the United States. You can ride to the top of the arch on a train that works like a Ferris wheel. Doesn't St. Louis look beautiful from the top? To the west you can see Busch Memorial Stadium. The St. Louis football team

Left: The Museum of Science and Industry in St. Louis
Above: Lindbergh's plane, the *Spirit of St. Louis*. Today,
airplanes and rocket ships are made in St. Louis.

plays there. The Cardinals play baseball there. To the

east, you can see boats on the Mississippi River.

St. Louis has some great museums. The Museum of

Westward Expansion (ex • PAN • shun), under the arch,

shows how the West was settled. Visit the Museum of

Science and Natural History. There you can learn about

ancient Indians, earthquakes, and the human body. The

Missouri Historical Society has a big exhibit on Charles

Lindbergh (LIND • berg). Lindbergh was the first to fly

an airplane alone across the Atlantic Ocean. Some St.

Louis people helped pay for his airplane. He called it the

Spirit of St. Louis.

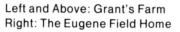
Left and Above: Grant's Farm
Right: The Eugene Field Home

Visit Grant's Farm in St. Louis. Ulysses (you • LISS • eez) S. Grant was born in Ohio, but he lived here for a time. In 1868 Ulysses S. Grant was elected 18th president of the United States.

The Eugene (YOU • jeen) Field house is also in St. Louis. Eugene Field lived here until he was six years old. Eugene Field became a children's poet. Did you ever hear of "the gingham dog and the calico cat"? Field wrote about them in his poem "The Duel." He also wrote "Wynken, Blynken, and Nod."

Just a few blocks away, visit the Old Courthouse on Fourth Street. The Dred Scott case was first heard in this tall building.

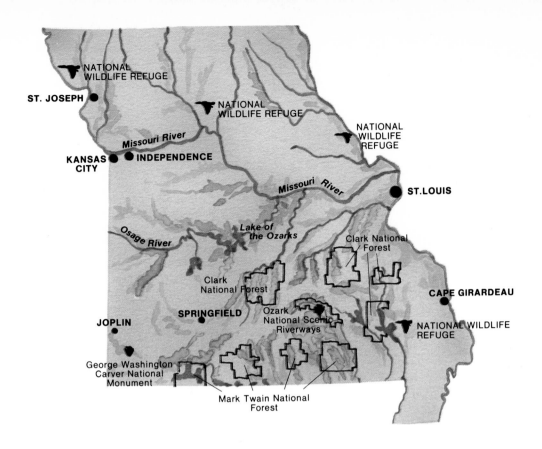

You can take a riverboat ride on the Mississippi River in St. Louis. In the 1800s, people traveled the river in boats like these. Today, boats on the river take St. Louis products to other cities.

Beer is a big St. Louis product. You can visit a brewery in the city. They'll show you how the grains are mashed to make beer. They'll show you how it is put in bottles. They won't let you drink it though—unless you're an adult!

Above: The governor's mansion in Jefferson City
Right: Meramec Caverns

At one time there were herds of elk and buffalo in
Missouri. Almost all of them were killed off. Near St.
Louis is a preserve where elk and buffalo live. It is called
Lone Elk Park. The animals there cannot be hunted.

Missouri has about 3,900 known caves—more than
any other state. Meramec Caverns (MARE • ah • mack
KAV • ernz) is about 60 miles southwest of St. Louis, at
Stanton. Millions of years ago, water carved out this
cave. Chemicals in dripping water formed weird rocks.

Jefferson City is about 128 miles west of St. Louis.
Jefferson City is the capital of Missouri. Lawmakers
wanted a capital near the center. They picked Jefferson
City in 1821, and it became capital in 1826.

28

Left: The state capitol building stands on a
hill near the Missouri River.
Above: Taum Sauk Mountain, the highest point
in Missouri

After seeing Jefferson City, head into southern
Missouri. The land gets hilly. Scientists call this hilly
area the Ozark Plateau. Most people call it the Ozark
Mountains.

Whichever you call it, the Ozarks are beautiful! You'll
see hills, rivers, and flower-filled valleys.

You'll also see forests in the Ozarks. The Mark Twain
National Forest is in southeastern Missouri. In all, about
one-third of Missouri is wooded. Oak, hickory, and ash
are just three kinds of trees you'll find. People enjoy
hiking in Missouri's forests. So do animals. You may see
deer peeking out at you from Ozark woodlands.

Ozark mountain people gave their towns interesting names. You'll see Blue Eye and Mountain Grove, Owls Bend, Romance, and Sleeper.

The people who came to the Ozarks in the 1800s learned to do things for themselves. They had to. They were out in the wilderness. There were no big-city stores nearby! They cut down trees and built log cabins. They made their own chairs, tables, and beds out of wood, too. To light their cabins they made beeswax candles. Women spun their own thread. Then they wove it into cloth.

Ozark mountain people made fiddles and banjos. They got together for "frolics." They danced to such tunes as the "Missouri Quickstep" and "Blue Mule."

A basket weaver in Silver Dollar City

Today, some Ozark people have maintained the crafts of days gone by. Visit Silver Dollar City, near Branson. Crafts festivals are held there. You can see how Ozark people made candles, baskets, and glass. At the Mountain Folks' Music Festival in Silver Dollar City you can hear the music of the hill people.

Springfield is the biggest city in southern Missouri. It is also the third biggest city in the state. In the 1820s Delaware Indians lived in the area. In about 1830, the Indians were forced to move. White settlers arrived.

Liberty Memorial in Kansas City

Near Springfield are many dairy farms. Milk, cream, and butter are packaged in Springfield. Wheat grown in the area is sent to Springfield. There it is made into flour. Trees in nearby forests are cut down. The lumber is made into furniture.

About 175 miles northwest of Springfield is the state's second biggest city. This is Kansas City, Missouri. It is just east of Kansas City, Kansas.

Once, Kansa Indians built their earth lodges in this area. Remember René Auguste Chouteau who helped found St. Louis? His nephew, Francois (fran • SWAZ) Chouteau, helped found Kansas City in 1821. It, too, began as a fur-trading post. In the 1880s, railroads helped Kansas City grow into a big shipping center.

The Harry S. Truman Sports Complex in Kansas City

Kansas City is near the center of the United States. It is nicknamed the *Heart of America*. Area farmers send wheat to Kansas City. There it is ground into flour. Frozen foods, cars, and chemicals are three other Kansas City products. These go by train from the Heart of America to other cities.

Visit the Nelson Gallery-Atkins Museum. It is a big art museum. There you can see paintings by famous artists. At the Kansas City Museum of History and Science you can learn about the stars and Osage Indians. The city also has a fine zoo and an orchestra.

Harry S. Truman Library

Kansas City—or K.C. as some call it—is a big sports city. The Royals play baseball in K.C. The Chiefs play football. The Kings are the basketball team.

Independence is just east of Kansas City. In the 1800s it was the *Gateway to the West*. Thousands of pioneers formed wagon trains on their way out West from here.

Visit the Harry S. Truman Library in Independence. There you can learn about our 33rd president.

St. Joseph is about 50 miles north of Independence. Over 100 years ago, the mail was sent by Pony Express. The Pony Express was a group of young men. One would ride for 75 miles. Then he handed the mail to the next

Left: The Pony Express stables in St. Joseph
Above: A statue showing the Pony Express rider

rider. By this relay method, the Pony Express took the mail all the way to California. The Pony Express stables can be seen in St. Joseph. From here, Pony Express riders began the 2,000-mile trip West.

Visit the Jesse James House, also in St. Joseph. You can see where the outlaw was shot down.

As you travel northeast from Independence you'll see many farms. You'll see wheat farms. You'll see fields of soybeans and corn. You'll see cows that give milk and cows that become roast beef. You'll see (and perhaps smell) hogs. Eggs and chickens are two other Missouri farm products.

In years past, mules from the Show Me State pulled plows and did other farm work. Now, machines do most of the work that Missouri mules once did.

Hannibal, in northeast Missouri, is a good place to finish your trip. A boy named Samuel Clemens (SAM • you • el KLEM • enz) grew up in Hannibal. He fished and went to school (when he wasn't playing hooky) in Hannibal. When Sam wanted to do something, he was very stubborn. "He's kin to a Missouri mule!" said his mother. He wanted to become a Mississippi riverboat

Mark Twain Home and Museum

36

Above: The Mark Twain Cave near Hannibal
Left: The Tom and Huck Statue in Hannibal

pilot. He became a good one. He later became a great writer and changed his name to Mark Twain. Mark Twain wrote *Tom Sawyer* and *Huckleberry Finn*.

Visit the Mark Twain Home and Museum in Hannibal. There you can see where this great writer lived.

The Mark Twain Cave is near Hannibal. As a boy, he explored this cave. Once he got lost there. In *Tom Sawyer*, Tom gets lost in this same cave.

Many other interesting people have lived in the Show Me State.

The George
Washington Carver
boyhood statue

George Washington Carver was born near Diamond
Grove in about 1859. His parents were slaves. As a boy,
George Washington Carver liked to grow plants. People
called him "the plant doctor." He worked his way
through college as a cook and a janitor. He became a
college teacher. Carver became famous for making
products out of plants. He made flour and candy from
sweet potatoes. He made soap, ink, and a kind of milk
from peanuts. He created new kinds of apples, plums,
pears, and cotton. The George Washington Carver
National Monument is in southwest Missouri. It honors
"the plant doctor" on the farm where he was born.

Martha Jane Canary was born in Princeton, Missouri,
in about 1852. She could ride a horse. She could shoot a

A statue of
General Pershing
in Laclede

gun. She became a scout when the army was fighting
Indians out West. She was known as "Calamity (kah •
LAM • ih • tee) Jane."

Nellie Tayloe Ross was another Missouri woman who
became famous out West. She was born in St. Joseph. In
1924, Nellie Tayloe Ross became the first woman
governor of a state. This was when she was living in
Wyoming. She later became head of the United States
Mint—the place where coins are made. Nellie Tayloe
Ross lived to be 100 years old.

General John J. Pershing (PURR • zhing) was born near
Laclede in 1860. He was in charge of United States
soldiers in Europe during World War I.

Omar N. Bradley was another great army general. He was born in Clark in 1893. During World War II, he commanded the biggest U.S. army ever—about one million men.

Charles Dillon Stengel (STEN • gull) was born in Kansas City, Missouri. Since he was from K.C., people called him "Casey" Stengel. Casey Stengel became a baseball player with a sense of humor. Once, he lifted his baseball cap while he was batting. A bird flew out. He later became manager of the New York Yankees. He won seven World Series as the Yankee manager.

A great baseball player, Yogi Berra, was born in St. Louis. Yogi was a New York Yankee catcher who could throw and hit. He holds the all-time record for World Series hits—71. He played on 10 World Series winning teams—more than any other player.

Above: A modern riverboat on the Mississippi
River
Left: Deer Park in Cassville

Walter Cronkite of St. Joseph became a radio
announcer. He also wrote for newspapers. Later he
became a television reporter.

Home to the Missouri Indians . . . French fur traders
. . . Harry S. Truman . . . and George Washington
Carver.

A state that produces airplanes . . . beer . . . shoes . . .
and spaceships.

A beautiful land of caves . . . hills . . . and rivers.

A leading farming state.

Land of the Gateway Arch and Mississippi riverboats.

This is Missouri—the Show Me State.

Facts About MISSOURI

Area—69,686 square miles (19th biggest state)

Greatest Distance North to South—284 miles

Greatest Distance East to West—308 miles

Border States—Iowa on the north; Illinois, Kentucky, and Tennessee on the east across the Mississippi River; Arkansas on the south; Oklahoma, Kansas, and Nebraska on the west.

Highest Point—1,772 feet above sea level (Taum Sauk Mountain)

Lowest Point—230 feet above sea level (along shores of St. Francis River)

Hottest Recorded Temperature—118° (occurred four different places in July of different years)

Coldest Recorded Temperature—Minus 40° (at Warsaw on February 13, 1905)

Statehood—Our 24th state, on August 10, 1821

Origin of Name Missouri—Named for the Missouri River and Missouri Indians; the word Missouri is thought to come from an Indian word meaning "town of the large canoes"

Capital—Jefferson City (1826)

Previous Capitals—St. Louis and St. Charles

Counties—114, plus independent city of St. Louis

U.S. Senators—2

U.S. Representatives—10

Electoral Votes—12

State Senators—34

State Representatives—163

State Song—"Missouri Waltz" by J.R. Shannon and John Valentine Eppel

State Motto—*Salus populi suprema lex esto* (Latin meaning "The welfare of the people shall be the supreme law")

Nicknames—The Show Me State, the Cave State, the Mother of the West

State Seal—Adopted in 1822

State Flag—Adopted in 1913

State Colors—Red, white, and blue

State Flower—Hawthorn

State Bird—Bluebird

State Tree—Flowering dogwood

State Rock—Mozarkite

State Mineral—Galena

Some Colleges and Universities—Cardinal Glennon College, Kansas City Art Institute, Lincoln University, University of Missouri, School of the Ozarks, St. Louis University, St. Mary's Seminary College, Stephens College, Washington University

Main Rivers—Mississippi and Missouri (these are the two largest rivers in the United States)

Some Other Rivers—White, Black, Osage, St. Francis, Big, Meramec, Blackwater, Current, Big Tarkio

Biggest Lake—Lake of the Ozarks (man-made)

Caves—About 3,900

National Forest—Mark Twain National Forest

State Forests—80

State Parks—39

Animals—Deer, squirrels, rabbits, foxes, skunks, beavers, muskrats, opossums, raccoons, mink, quail, geese, wild turkeys, ducks, hawks, owls, rattlesnakes, copperheads, turtles

Fishing—Bass, catfish, bluegills, crappies, trout, perch, sunfish, jack salmon

Farm Products—Soybeans, corn, oats, barley, alfalfa, popcorn, strawberries, grapes, beef cattle, milk, hogs, eggs, chickens, turkeys

Mining—Lead, limestone, coal, oil

Manufacturing Products—Airplanes, cars, trains, space capsules, other transportation equipment, flour, beer, butter, cheese, other food products, chemicals, electrical machinery, furniture and other wood products, shoes, clothes, bricks, glass products, cement

Population—4,763,000 (1975 estimate)

Major Cities— St. Louis   489,000   (all 1979 estimates)
              Kansas City   438,000
              Springfield   134,000
              Independence   109,700
              St. Joseph   76,700
              Florissant   73,800

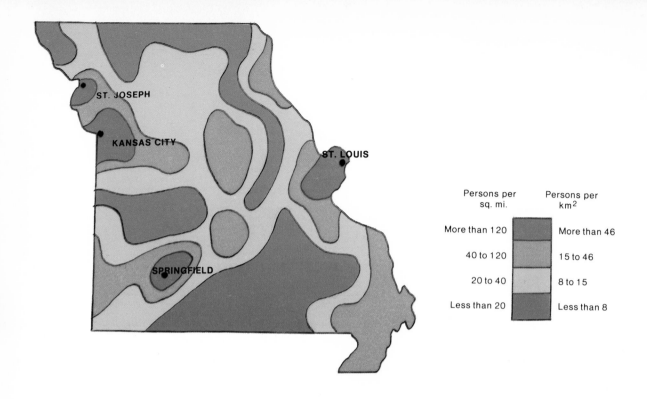

Persons per sq. mi. | Persons per km²
More than 120 | More than 46
40 to 120 | 15 to 46
20 to 40 | 8 to 15
Less than 20 | Less than 8

Missouri History

The first people came to Missouri at least 10,000 and possibly even 25,000
years ago.

1541—Spaniard De Soto possibly explores area

1673—Frenchmen Marquette and Joliet are known to explore Missouri

1682—French explorer La Salle claims big area, including Missouri, for
France

1693—Frenchmen have begun trading with Indians for furs by now

1700—Mission of St. Francis Xavier is built near St. Louis

1715—Lead is mined in southeastern Missouri

1735—About this time Ste. Genevieve (oldest town in Missouri) is founded

1762—Spain takes control, but French fur traders remain in Missouri

1763—Pierre Laclède picks site for fur-trading post (future St. Louis)

1764—Fourteen-year-old René Auguste Chouteau begins building St. Louis

1774—First Missouri school is founded at St. Louis

1799—Daniel Boone is one of many American pioneers arriving in Missouri

1800—Missouri is again under French control

1803—By Louisiana Purchase, Missouri becomes part of United States

1804—President Jefferson sends Lewis and Clark to explore

1811-1812—New Madrid earthquakes

1812—Missouri Territory is formed by U.S. Congress

1812-1815—Indian Wars; most of beaten Indians are forced out of Missouri

1819—Arkansas Territory is formed from Missouri Territory

1820—About 56,000 whites, 10,000 black slaves, and 6,000 Indians live in
Missouri Territory

1820—Missouri Compromise admits Maine as a Free State, declares where
slavery will be allowed, and provides for Missouri entering Union as a
Slave State

1821—On August 10, 1821, Missouri becomes the 24th state!

1826—Jefferson City becomes the capital of the new state

1829—René Auguste Chouteau dies 65 years after he helped found St. Louis

1830—About 140,000 people live in state of Missouri

1835—Samuel Clemens (Mark Twain) is born in Florida, Missouri; he soon
moves to Hannibal

1839—University of Missouri is founded at Columbia

1840s—Pioneers, heading Westward, depart from Missouri

1857—In Dred Scott Decision, Supreme Court says slaves are just property

1861-1865—During Civil War, 109,000 Missouri men fight for Northern army;
many Civil War battles in Missouri

1870—Steamboat *Robert E. Lee* beats *Natchez* in race from New Orleans to
St. Louis

1880—Population of state has jumped to 2,168,380

1882—Jesse James is shot down at his house in St. Joseph

1884—On May 8, Harry S. Truman is born at Lamar

1904—World's Fair is held at St. Louis

1910—Mark Twain, one of the greatest American writers, dies

1914-1918—During World War I, Missourian John J. Pershing leads American troops in Europe; 140,257 Missourians serve during this war

1921—Happy 100th birthday, Show Me State!

1927—Charles Lindbergh flies across Atlantic Ocean in the *Spirit of St. Louis*

1931—Bagnell Dam, forming Lake of the Ozarks, is completed

1939-1945—During World War II, General Omar Bradley of Missouri commands one million soldiers; 450,000 Missouri men and women serve during this war

1945—Harry S. Truman of Independence becomes the 33rd president when President Franklin D. Roosevelt dies

1948—Truman is elected on his own

1965—Gateway Arch is completed

1967—St. Louis Cardinals win the World Series for the eighth time

1970—Population of Show Me State is 4,677,399

1970s—Kansas City and St. Louis begin projects to improve run-down areas

1972—President Truman dies and is buried at Independence

1976—Republicans hold their convention at Kansas City

1977—Joseph P. Teasdale begins serving as the state's 48th governor

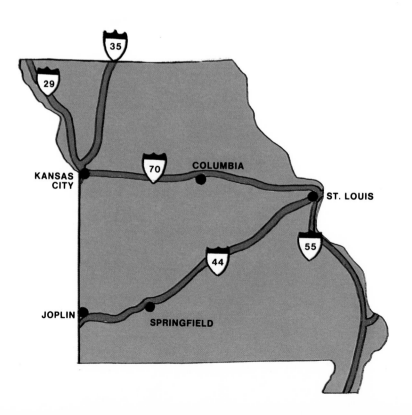

INDEX

INDEX, Cont'd

About the Author:

Dennis Fradin attended Northwestern University on a creative writing scholarship and graduated in 1967. While still at Northwestern, he published his first stories in *Ingenue* magazine and also won a prize in *Seventeen's* short story competition. A prolific writer, Dennis Fradin has been regularly publishing stories in such diverse places as *The Saturday Evening Post, Scholastic, National Humane Review, Midwest,* and *The Teaching Paper.* He has also scripted several educational films. Since 1970 he has taught second grade reading in a Chicago school—a rewarding job, which, the author says, "provides a captive audience on whom I test my children's stories." Married and the father of three children, Dennis Fradin spends his free time with his family or playing a myriad of sports and games with his childhood chums.

About the Artists:

Len Meents studied painting and drawing at Southern Illinois University and after graduation in 1969 he moved to Chicago. Mr. Meents works full time as a painter and illustrator. He and his wife and child currently make their home in LaGrange, Illinois.

Richard Wahl, graduate of the Art Center College of Design in Los Angeles, has illustrated a number of magazine articles and booklets. He is a skilled artist and photographer who advocates realistic interpretations of his subjects. He lives with his wife and two sons in Libertyville, Illinois.